Points of Recognition

Also by Jane Williams and published by Ginninderra Press
My Nan Speaks Nanish
Oskar Saves the Day
Echoes of Flight
Parts of the Main
Begging the Question

Jane Williams
Points of Recognition

Acknowledgements

Antipodes (Australian and New Zealand literature), *Eureka Street, Live Encounters, Barren Magazine, Asimov's Science Fiction Magazine, Tincture Journal, Echidna Tracks, Acorn, Wales Haiku Journal, Tiny Words, Daily Haiga,* Australian Catholic University Prize for Poetry, 2018 (3rd place), Australian Haiku Society 2018 Spring Haiga Kukai (1st place and highly commended), 2017 Woorilla Poetry Prize (1st place)

For careful reading of the manuscript, my thanks to Lyn Reeves and Sarah Day, with special thanks to Lyn for taking the time to illuminate the connections between the haiku and longer poems. To Ron C. Moss for permission to use his gorgeous feather image for the cover. I'm grateful to Chen-ou Liu for translating some of the haiku into Chinese and to the haiku group Watersmeet for their fellowship. I'm indebted to my publisher Stephen Matthews for his continued support of my work, to John Johnson for our enriching poetry exchange and to Ralph Wessman as always, for his sustaining love and faith.

Points of Recognition
ISBN 978 1 76109 080 6
Copyright © text Jane Williams 2021
Cover image: Ron C. Moss

First published 2021 by
GINNINDERRA PRESS
PO Box 3461 Port Adelaide 5015 Australia
www.ginninderrapress.com.au

Contents

Introduction	7
In praise of the rituals of others	11
When women share their stories with other women	13
This isn't a poem about eggs	15
38 minutes later	17
All manner of thing	19
Orienteering	22
She dreams of leaving his country – 1963	24
After reading about breast-ironing	26
Little thieves	28
The Dogs of Cat City	30
Suspension of disbelief	33
Life imitating poetry	36
Lists	38
Love is not in the air	41
Mrs M	44
A tribute to knees	47
Inheritance	49
Flight	52
3 points of recognition	54
Pancake theorem	58
The Letter	60
The world gifted back to itself	63
Unexpected intimacy	66
A plea from Koschei the Deathless	68
Largesse	71
Cause and effect	74
A short history of the smile	77
The white tufted air	80
Meeting the man from the future	82

Surviving your imagined death	84
(I) Confirm humanity	87
Simply 21	89
Diversional therapy	92
How it ends and begins	95
Men I have worked for	97
Bringing the world home	100
The naming	103
The facts of our lives	105
Letting in the neighbour	108
Present tense	111
I try to not write a pandemic poem and fail	114
Like Alice letting go	116

Introduction

Points of Recognition is a collection that is concerned with what it means to be alive, to be connected to others: friends, family, strangers. It celebrates difference and diversity of lifestyle and cultures with exuberance, affinity and rapport.

The title is taken from Williams's prize-winning poem '3 Points of recognition'. 'Empathy' was the theme of that year's Australian Catholic University Prize for Poetry and, in fact, empathy is the hallmark of Williams's writing, and of this book.

Interspersed between the poems are haiku, another genre in which Williams excels. These small poems have their roots in the traditional seventeen-onji poems of Japan. The contemporary, westernised practice known as English-language Haiku (ELH) uses far fewer syllables but retains many of the features of the Japanese haiku, including the ability to communicate, in a few well-chosen words, something that is both personal and, at the same time, universal. The Japanese poet, Yoshika Yoshino, describes haiku in this way:

> A condensed capsule of poetry, haiku contains explosive energy and has, therefore, the possibility of becoming symbolic verse that can explicate universal, cosmic truths.

It is recommended that haiku be read slowly and reflectively, allowing the imagery and its associations to evoke a larger picture than is first apparent. In their brevity and conciseness, haiku resemble an ink-brush painting where minimal strokes suggest the subject, leaving the viewer to fill in what is left out. The surrounding white space says as much as the lines do. Each reader will bring her own references and experiences to the completion of the haiku poem.

The pairings of the longer poem and the haiku that follows it is not accidental. The two forms, which effectively stand alone and complete in themselves, are subtly linked in the sequencing of *Points of Recognition* by an idea, image or feeling. They play against each other in a way that lends an extra dimension to both. This arrangement bears a resemblance to a related form of Japanese writing, the haibun, a prose piece followed by a brief verse that communicates with the prose in an understated, indirect way.

Take for example the opening poem, 'In praise of the rituals of others', where we encounter the diversity of characters who inhabit the margins of the poet's world, but for whom she feels great thankfulness for their being there in spite of the lack of privacy it might afford her. The last few lines give special thanks for the sounds rising from Apartment One, where a new daughter is being welcomed into the world. We surmise from the mention of ululation and the fragrance of spiced tea that this is an immigrant family.

The haiku that follows, when read in conjunction with the poem, expands on the glimpse we have been given into the neighbours' life,

> Boxing Day sales
> my neighbour's early start
> stacking shelves

It is not unusual to find immigrants who have come from professional backgrounds and who are unable to find work in their fields, working in unskilled jobs such as trolley collectors at supermarkets, cleaners and shelf-stackers. This haiku adds not only an extra layer of depth to Williams's observations but a feeling of empathy and an acknowledgement of the difficulties as well as the joys that are common to us all.

Just as each poem and each haiku elicits a sense of recognition between writer and reader, the poem and the haiku interrelate. 'When women share their stories with other women' also speaks of shared bonds and roads travelled. The haiku that links back to this poem

> early snowmelt
> I turn the teapot
> three times each way

alludes to the poet's own cultural background and the customs that have been passed down through the lineage of women in her life.

This play between genres is evident throughout the book – take, for example, a poem about piecing together a jigsaw puzzle followed by a haiku about joining the dots, and 'Inheritance', where a poem that mentions an uncle's cancer is followed by a haiku that speaks of the transience of our own life span. Family memories, observations of strangers, world events, the consolation of beauty to be found in the everyday are all material to be transformed by Williams's curiosity and compassion into reflections on our shared humanity and the interconnectedness of everything in this world where we are fellow-travellers.

Points of Recognition is a book of wonder, born of the poet's wonderings ('Let it be said / I never stopped wondering') that contains within it not just the wonder that is curiosity and genuine interest in life, the planet, perfect strangers, human longings and foibles, but also wonder in the sense of awe that we should be a part of it all. I am grateful to Jane Williams for being 'hardwired to respond' to even the smallest moments that evoke an understanding and joyful acceptance of the many points of recognition between ourselves and others, and for the beauty of the poetry through which she expresses and elucidates her response.

Lyn Reeves
Vice-President, Australian Haiku Society

In praise of the rituals of others

Today I frosted the kitchen window because
before it finds the mountain through the glass
door of the balcony it must pass through
our shared hallway and the new neighbours
are moving in just as we'd started to befriend
the old ones. There is nothing to hide but the usual
human foibles and vanities but we have learned
privacy by rote all our westernised lives
and can be driven to distraction by our own
self-view. So thank God for the rituals of others,
the unofficial town criers and underseers
of business as usual. Disrupters of complacency
and conviction. Thank God for the shift worker
laundering at 3 a.m., the self-talker shooing
imaginary unwanted guests with nothing
more than the thinning straw of a broom.
Thank God for Bollywood and daytime TV.
For the all night partyers and marathon
love makers. For the hash brownie bakers,
the nut crackers and pot stirrers.
And yes even the drum-beating banjo-twanging
wannabe musicians. But special thanks, God,
for the incense wafting up from the first floor
through our bathroom vent; frankincense
I'm tempted to think on this particular day
discovering the tonal shifts and rapid firing
of water through old pipes is in glorious fact
the ululation of women at the door of number 1
where a daughter is newly born and Lipton tea
is spiced with cardamom and cinnamon and
the curtains are seldom drawn.

Boxing Day sales
my neighbour's early start
stacking shelves

When women share their stories with other women

Dust falls from crystal balls
everywhere. Empty fields
signed beware of the bull
call out memory's bluff
as one by one old selves
old beliefs are drawn forth
shrugged off not without
compassion. A window box
over the Atlantic encourages
bees and daydreams. White hair
sings in streaks of peated whisky.
When women share their stories
with other women greyscale lifts
from the world's face revealing
borders crossed and recrossed
a chroma of microgravity
spherical candle flames
the gaze returned in kind
in renewed and fearless
recognition.

early snowmelt
I turn the teapot
three times each way

This isn't a poem about eggs

but growing up we learned to walk
on their shells. If our family was a circus

then my father was the ringmaster.
We slipped our knots while he slept

becoming limbo dancers and funambulists
clowning around the borderlines.

This isn't a poem about eggs but with six
kids, a house cow and a surplus of pancakes

it seemed we were always racing for the first
or reaching for the last of anything.

This isn't a poem about eggs though the line
I recall the most often from *Angela's Ashes*

is Malachy McCourt asking what a man
would be doing with a whole one to himself.

This isn't a poem about eggs but if it was
it might try to describe the way they are shaped

for safe landing, the joy of watching one crack
from the inside.

heat storm
just a drip
from the kitchen tap

38 minutes later

false   alarm

in black on white in giant orange pixels
across phone screens across highway lanes
the new message repeated until credible then
actual *there is no threat* and still and yet
the slow and wary return to calm
hurricane kits put back into storage along
with plans to revisit and revise strangers
leaving the homes of other strangers their
temporary connections sparking like faulty
wiring or the perfect one night stand
bathtubs drained of drinking water razors
removing duct tape from windows children
hoisted urban myth wise from storm drains
and manholes abandoned cars reclaimed
and redirected tourists shocked from postcards
the seal broken on a 21 year old bottle
of Hibiki whisky its price tagging time
wasted keeping up appearances an auto
corrected tweet turns *missile* to *muscle*
the emergency service shift worker's nightmared
finger on the button state of the art
computer asking *are you sure are you sure you
want to do this?* that mushrooming nanosecond
between the known world and the world
starting over

screen time
no time to process
world news

All manner of thing

'... all shall be well, and all shall be well, and all manner of thing shall be well.' – Julian of Norwich

Even those times when nothing seems
as it used or ought –

the sugar fixes of childhood dissolve
under an avalanche of predestined falls:
Tooth Fairy, Easter Bunny, Santa Claus ...

The chasm of longing for more deepens
as sacrifice becomes virtuous then ravenous
confessing nothing up the sleeve
but the nub of a wished-for wing bud;
to skate earth's patina, printless, shyly
hopeful of a place among the stars.

Even as the decades snowball
and family gatherings strain to accommodate
the estranged or partially or wholly missing.

No sweetener sweet enough, no holy water
or firewater pure enough to clear the malaise.

Even when the most perverse reverse
Tinkerbell Effect takes hold
the harder the wish the more impenetrable
the divide, banks of cloud heavy as vintage
Swiss army blankets.

Even then, even now, how life
and its everyday miracle insists.

See there! Pacific gull fishing a streak of yellow
peaked red and dipping in and out of view.
And there! Little burnt orange boat, its sky blue sail
unfurling, gathering momentum…

with each cry
of the bush stone-curlew
night deepens

Orienteering

I have finally begun the Ravensburger 1000-piece jigsaw depicting a shelf stacked askew with books whose titles playfully misrepresent their author's intent. My favourites: *The magpie who came in from the cold*, *Much ado about knitting*, *The great brain robbery*, *The moon and six pens* and the fantastically romantic *Last UFO in Paris*.

Of my actual books, too many marked for finishing with souvenir bookmarks – bamboo etched in peasantry, the irreverence of dog-earing.

The woollen slipper I knitted for a long-footed friend, sky-blue, sun-striped, its partner completed and gifted months back along with a sheepish IOU.

Drafts of letters to imagined patrons arguing the equal market weight of the potato and the poem.

In speaking out loud I often manage only half sentences, each one trailing off, stymied by permutation.

And just now trying to blink back the books missing from the top right hand corner, I discover…apple trees, hill tops, this taunting piece of sky…

starry sky
all grown-up still
joining the dots

She dreams of leaving his country – 1963

I dream it this way. We will leave
his country with its thick skinned skies,
the toil of making frayed ends meet.
Let someone else eat every part
of the pig but its grunt. Where I'm from
oranges are no more exotic than potatoes
and sunshine softens even the hardest
edge of longing. That's where we'll settle.
Wed before I'm showing; those first few weeks
struck from the calendar, wallpapered over
in pea-green and saffron. No family
but a few close, close-mouthed friends.
How we'll laugh at TV's The Housewife
of the Year as if the joke could be on anyone
but us, anyone but me. Buckley's.
Instead we will learn how to cook together
inventive dishes with unguessable origins.
This will be the beginning. Good luck to us.
I will translate Bodgies and Widgies, teach him
how to jive. He will sing the baby asleep and me
awake, the lilt of his voice only ever tender.
Our children will love and outlive us.
Sorry for your troubles never reaching our ears,
our hearts, never once meant for us.

ocean voyage
the slow movement
of sea stars

After reading about breast-ironing

I recall our 1980s high school nurse throwing her daughter
a Period Party. How we mocked the idea, the handmade
invitations, attempting to cool acute embarrassment, conceal
our small confused envy.

We were the girls of conservative women who discreetly left
pamphlets on bedroom dressers. If we were lucky, a packet
of pads buried deep in the bottom drawer.

Decades later a friend confesses as a girl she knew nothing
so that when the time came she believed she was bleeding
to death. To death.

On the rag. Aunty Flo. That time of the month.

These days when my youngest steps out to Reclaim the Night
I admit to a fearful pride.

Is it any wonder some mothers keep vigilant watch,
press heavy heated stones against nubs of breasts against
unwanted attention, clinging to such sad and dangerous
falsehoods as boys being somehow easier to grow,
as bruises that simply come and go.

first strokes
of my grandchild's face
twelve-week scan

Little thieves

Too rodent-like to test the grounds
of my dreams until I am gifted this copy
of Lady with Ermine. A study in nuanced
movement; the index finger of her right hand
flexed mid-caress along the animal's snowy
neckline.

Depicted in profile, both sets of eyes angled
expectantly as if toward opposing notions
of rescue and escape.

I learn new creature habits. Sleeping
up to eighteen hours a day. Waking
to new scents; all variations on the same
theme – essence of time. Sociability is everything.
Touch. Secreting away titbits for the afterlife.
Adept at running amuck. What's not to love?

I am compelled to hang the print
in full view of my comings and goings
as if for all our sakes.

One morning power walking through
the neighbourhood I am slowed by the raw
plea of a homemade poster peeling
from a street pole; a monochrome face
emerging from a darker background familiar
as any promised broken land of domesticity.

Sasha beloved ferret
Missing
From the Big Blue house

rainy day
little handprints
on the sky

The Dogs of Cat City

If I were a dog or a cat person
I would probably be a cat person but
I am neither. You could say I'm simply
an admirer of Nature's work in general.
Dogs however, find me stepping
gingerly to one side. A psychologist friend
of a friend says this could be a trust issue.
Also, in their company I am often guilt-edged
and some prodigal version of homesick.

Today I am in Cat City where I find only dogs.

Here's one now, rounding the hotel corner;
a medium sized collarless mutt loping along
followed by another and another …
They are uniformly black-brown except for
the jigsawed one which could be
but probably isn't a miniature Friesian cow.

Soon they have multiplied and my susceptible mind
has quantified and qualified them into a pack.

When I google the pack dogs of cat city
I am led to council initiatives:
Capture-Neuter-Vaccinate-Return and
Operation Roaming Dog Removal.

If I dwell on these I am sure to become
more than a little fearful. I am sure to recall
the rabid details of Stephen King's Cujo.
But such projected fear is outweighed
by even the kernel of real and present
sorrow. Poor dogs – unwitting scavengers
in the wastelands of our fair-weather friendships.

For the lucky ones adopted into the House
of Human, there are bones aplenty
and a diggable yard it takes long enough
to circle. Some live to see a boy through
boyhood, are loved truly, that is, beyond
measure. They foster, in return
a discerning sense of smell and fair play,
of when the moment calls for nothing less
than the gleeful chase of a ball.

The blessed few of course, untamed,
untamable, roam the mountain ranges
and desertscapes of parallel worlds,
howling their homes into being. Each night
dreaming of the hunt and (why not
in this version?) creatures mythic as man.

dog park
sunlit every body
off leash

Suspension of disbelief

At sixty-five my bachelor uncle
gave up smoking six months
before his bypass and wonders
tongue in cheek if there's a link.

He tells me this over the phone.
We haven't spoken in 14 years
because life happens we tell ourselves.

I tell him I remember how
he introduced me to Harry Chapin
when I was still in my teens and cats
in the cradle were all the metaphor
I needed for the world's sorrows.

How he once took his girl on a double date
after the car accident but before
her face had been fully reconstructed
and his mate wanted to know what happened
and he told him in detail then casually asked
So…what's your date's excuse?

What I don't mention is that Christmas
he walked out, disappeared, reemerging
well into the new year as if he'd just been
to the corner shop for cigarettes.

How as time rumoured on through affairs
of the heart, one loan shark too many
I crafted my own version of events –

Some kindly alien abduction,
no invasive probing just a few
randomised questions about life
as he/we knew it.

Aussie rules, TV dinners,
what it means to outlive your brother
then your sister. The countless ways
we've come up with to enhance
and numb the senses.

Then before we even noticed
his absence, he'd be returned to us
absentmindedly stroking his beard,
heart in a state of permanent ceasefire,
memory and his slate wiped clean.

overcast
the fluffed-up kookaburra
holds his laugh

Life imitating poetry

How else are we to believe in her?
This girl nestled in the branches
of a weeping willow,
only her bare legs visible.
She is singing an aria (we're certain of it)
on this spring evening
by the walking track overlooking
the bay where small white boats
test their moorings in the breeze
and the scent of daphne reaches us
somewhere between middle and high
C and we are silenced by the emptiness
of the sky and this longing to fill it
with our own song of kinship.
Nearby a fisherman
is gently dehooking and returning
his catch of the day;
perhaps this is an embellishment
but not the girl or the music.
Not the way the water ripples
and the leaves shiver
their symbiotic assent…

mud map
all roads lead to
childhood

Lists

He makes them under
doctor's orders
warding off
a disappearing self.

Long walks keep pace
with silent recitations.

The periodic table
a lullaby
of configuration
and recurrence.

First names
of prime ministers
and on a clear day
their pets.

88 constellations
tempt moments of fancy
difficult not to inhabit:
Centaurus galloping
head in the stars,
the wings of Aquila
soaring through
the dome of the known

but heel toe, left right
he returns to terra firma
all wayward thoughts
dissolved on impact.

At times his doggedness
mistaken for genius
makes the humour of his day.

Repeating the exercise
ad infinitum
he takes comfort
in pure method,
placing his faith in
the mind's ball and chain
combination lock,
something up the sleeve,
the lady sawn in half
wriggling at both ends
and the disappeared
almost always returning.

music therapy
that moment his mother
remembers him

Love is not in the air

but in the way
we try to shape it
tunnelling through
the rubble of language.
Reaching.

In the work we do
growing into

the spaces we create,

the silences we invite
to be
at home in the world.

Again and again
in the generational act
of mend and make-do.

Incremental bridging
of colossal divides.

In resisting the fall.
In falling.

In the equal measure
we give hold and release.

How we offer and welcome
reverential intentional touch.

And in the uncommon sense
of two sisters from a family
of refugees travelling home

together   alone

having done the math
and reasoned love's cost –

if one plane crashes
only one child will be lost.

waning crescent
this urge to touch
everything

Mrs M

At her service I learn things
about the mother of my childhood friend.

How her keen sense for missing pieces
(the dog walking past without the boy by his side)
saved the neighbour's son from drowning.

The way the single-mindedness of her love
hunted down the only meds that could keep
her shell-shocked husband at home.

And that lakeside family holiday;
laughing so hard her teeth flew out and into
the water, her daughters diving after them
in comedic horror, while she kept on
kept on laughing.

Nonagenarian, immodestly sharing
the Queen's birthday.

It seemed to me through the decades she kept
her family fortified with bottomless cups of tea,
lavishly buttered toast. There was always a cat
called Puss. A tree swing in the backyard.
Ever the pragmatist; a career in nursing
fostered imagination as a means to an end.

Tougher than I remember, no doubt
but she had this way of winking like
she was having an in-joke with God
and if you played your cards right
she might put in a good word.

And now I am gifted her hatchback;
two decades of just fifty thousand clicks between
church and the grandkids and line dancing.

In its cooling engine reverberations of flight.
It is the colour of mermaids. Of kryptonite.

day centre
all smiles for the cat
on her hat

A tribute to knees

Largest joints in the human body
hinged to swing a hundred
and fifty degrees.

Their crawl before you walk life
lesson never again applied
with such fervent attention to detail
such faith in the plan.

The backs of them in classrooms –
one girl's in particular,
the way they blinked in and out of view
as she sat and rose and could almost
drown a boy in their milky hollows.

Countless Saturdays in the confessional box
reciting lists of peccadillos while deeper
truths ached not unpleasantly beneath
the calloused armour of our patellae.

Indelibly marked by childhood skirmish.
Oh the run, skip, hop and jump of them,
landing only ever a prelude to takeoff ...

realignment
between hip replacements
new dance steps

Inheritance

At the end of a good enough day
dreaming blood oranges and all the warmth
they conjure. Maybe a finely tuned tin whistle.

My grandmother weighted under daub and thatch
stretched meals into parlour tricks.
Ruling with a hand as quick as her eye was sharp.
She allowed me to plait and coil her long-enough-to-
sit-on hair into evening pinwheels
igniting and spiralling the imagined life of Riley.
Advising prayers to the Father be sent always
through the Mother.

The grandfather I never met found in himself,
post-war, a cleverness with numbers and a proclivity
to press a coin into any upturned palm.
Still waters ran to yearly benders.
He grew vegetables and chickens for the table
when he wasn't wishing himself away with the fairies
and out to sea. When he wasn't lying low
loaning out his medal come Remembrance Day.

An inheritance of intangibles:
Warring gods and the saving grace of dreams.
Starlight travelling through time just to reach us. Us.
Peat fires and before that the scent of freshly turned earth.

What is there to unwish that would have brought me
elsewhere. Had I fallen in love say with maths instead
of poetry, favoured reason over the heart's wayward tug.

More than enough that my own children see past
the politics of jutting jaws to clear and inclusive resolve.
Their gold-flecked eyes unwavering
as they cultivate a knack for deciphering babble.
For knowing the right thing to say to an uncle as the last
of his hair is shaved in that final unwinnable race.
Such a lovely shaped skull. Priceless the smile
that retrieved the vanity from his one crooked tooth.

family tree
my footprint in the dust
by the window

Flight

Lead back to the first
brine-laced breath,
reticulated pattern of
light and dark. I cannot
distinguish myself from
this haphazard weave
of underscrub. Always
on point of taking root
or turning back when
some demigod scatters
luminous breadcrumbs
at my feet and I am
(despite my grown-up
years my sensible shoes)
off again
far-fetched and hapless
groupie to the stars ...

spring breeze
how many more years
my itchy feet

3 points of recognition

*Is the miracle that we can bear to see each other at all
that we do not freeze in the stark clarity of reflection or
spontaneously combust in the transient rapture of being?*

1

One inexplicably melancholic lunch break
from a job she neither loves nor hates
a young woman (once the girl most likely)
enters a café and asks for her usual
(hazelnut latte extra shot full cream).
The barista, noticing some subtle change
in demeanor; the unset jaw perhaps or
a certain resignation in each breath and blink
refrains from their routine exchange,
forgoes the standard Rosetta
and in a tone suggesting more
than a welcome back to the hive
whispers *today*
today I make for you this…
Now decades on eyes closed
she can still see the impossibly detailed
feathers feel the lick of flames in the tease
of an updraft.

2

Clancy at the door is saying *yes
just like the poem* he gets that a lot
and with his fresh shave strawberry
blonde curls and lilting accent
he knows he could be the poster boy
for Garda Síochána na hÉireann
or the reformation of priesthood.
His smile is solid as the equal armed
red cross embossed on his T-shirt.
Once a clipboard and tin can man
did the job now it's all iPads and
credit cards. He reminds each resident
in the carbon copy block
one in five report a symptom
of mental illness
and it all goes like clockwork
until one of them asks not unkindly
and yourself Clancy?

3

In the early hours of a near perfect autumn day
a gentle breeze rolling leaves between the houses
of a hushed suburb a woman stands in her driveway
car door ajar about to get in or having just got out
answering the upbeat jingle of her mobile
and a passer-by (let's say a jogger) glancing over
notices the stiletto heels and thinks *how?*
when unexpectedly as if some bored director
flipped a switch the scene changes;
the woman's mouth a slow motion opening
emits a strange guttural hurt animal sound
as she doubles over in the kind of pain
the jogger (who is now the witness) knows
from experience can only be the jagged firing
of the starter's gun of grief.
The phone clamped to her ear now a lifeline
for as long as she doesn't let go
for as long as she continues to keen
monosyllabic disbelief.

hand extended
the homeless man asks
if I'm OK

Pancake theorem

When I find myself in doubt
a wise friend advises
Lie back and think of pancakes.

Once upon a stone age…

cattails and ferns were mixed
with water and baked on hot rocks.

Epochs on the Elizabethans enhanced
the palate with sherry and rosewater.

Twentieth century Catholicism favoured
lemon and a liberal sprinkling of sugar.

By the time I reach the parlours floating
buttery stacks through the caramelised air

I am returned to my senses and the gift
of accepting each day as it arrives;
flat-packed, some assemblage required,
choosing to believe whatever is left
over or missing ensures the continuum.

Sometimes the only way to neutralize
the mind's trickery is to hole up awhile
in a corner of the knowable world –

surrender to the elemental
comfort of its thingness.

old recipes
the careful measure
of pinch and dash

The Letter

A rare one these days from my mother who mastered social
media before me. Learning in her sixties to text like a teen,
abbreviating the world in tiny bytes. *All the better to travel through
cyberspace, to travel light* she might say. But not today. Today
there's this letter ambiguous as the view from my kitchen
window; the peak of mountain, clouds at their springtime
moodiest, long wet grass. A rainy day minus the rain. A day
of stasis. Of inwardness. A good day for stocktaking or
soul searching. For opening and reading snail mail. Inside
the envelope, two unwritten postcards, images she thought
might take my fancy. One a painted kaleidoscope of colour;
a bull's head tattooed between a woman's breasts. The other
a black and white photograph; an old man nursing a pint,
one bar stool over, a small child clutching a bag of crisps.
My mother knows adaptation is the key, that the heart can
inhabit more than one life. Still, she believes some things
are best served with pen in hand, a careful measure of time
through ink on paper. Faintly ruled paper, centre folded.
In the top left hand corners trademark numerals underscored.
Her looping cursive slants right like rows of trees shaped
by wind. Then somewhere between talk of food and wine,
adventure and settling down, the question of where, when
the time comes, to scatter my parents' ashes.
His in the Inch Abbey and out to sea. A return to roots.
For her any body of water will do. A tidal pool perhaps.
Any storm in a port. This woman. This man. Different breeds
of the same love. How ever have they managed – worlds apart –
their life? Through my kitchen window: mountain, clouds,

grass, not quite as I left them. Nothing ever wholly
as we leave it. If we're lucky or blessed someone else
to draw the longing from our story, hold it up to catch
the fading benevolent light.

hard to read
Mum's cursive loops
her last wishes

The world gifted back to itself

A tractor is levelling the beach
erasing yesterday's tourist tracks
and because its driver in his wisdom
finds no sense or joy in separating
the hum of the engine from the hum
of the sea caressing the edge of the world
he is also able to divine in the tyre prints
such marvels as the migration of birds
flying backward through time.

Further along a runner stops and drops
to a squat just long enough to mark out
a small grid above the tideline and
a near-perfect circle in its centre square.

A father plays chasings with his small children
zigzagging in and out of reach until their laughter
collides bringing them down in a circus tumble of
good to be alive, smiles stuck fast with
incalculable grains of sand.

A boy sits cross-legged by the water's edge
head bent and willing (surely this
is his super power) the water to flip
the belly-up fish back to life.

A husband photographs his wife knee-deep
in breaking waves, the lenses of his rheumy eyes
blinking her in and out of focus. Perhaps they
have been married a long time, long before
the fickle fashion of it. Perhaps he re-remembers
each year her wedding dress once white taking on
all the colours and contours of the ocean bed,
the light in her eyes angling, still angling him
home.

golden hour
sulphur-crested cockatoos
comb the sky

Unexpected intimacy

We might guess recognition occurred on the platform,
movie-wise, waiting for the train; half-waves perhaps,
hands almost reaching to remove ear buds, tilted
elsewhere smiles. Not quite a prelude to courtship,
each sedated by the romance of their own theme music.

But once seated, opposite and as it happens, face to face,
this acknowledgment; attending the same philosophy lecture
earlier that day has given them carte blanche to skip
the small talk and ask the big question in person in public

who is lonelier
the turtle or the fish?

One argues the turtle certainly, a solitary creature
for whom physical connection is a maintenance issue:
body temperature, breeding.

The other insists, the fish, doomed always to travel
in schools, a life of endless reflection craving contrast.

On and on back and forth until their quiet debate
reaches an impasse and the light from their eyes seems
to refract, to shimmer mirage-like in the air between them.

And those of us who are close enough to catch it
are also moved, surprised by an unexpected intimacy;
without so much as exchanging names, here we are, the ones
who are left, approaching together alone, the end of the line.

seasonal shadows
each year more and less
ourselves

A plea from Koschei the Deathless

I have long since forgotten
any previous existence.
Any given name
once cooed
in a mother's lovespeak.

But I crave it now.

I am hollowed by eternity,
by this shape-shifter's
half-life.
Ravaged by my appetite
for substance.

So fearful of the end
I created my own
version
of Matryoshka dolls;
protectors of my
endless days.

I beg you now dear
sympathetic reader,
find the loophole.
Free me.
Come closer and
I will tell you how.

My secret self
is buried
on an island
under a mighty tree
inside a box of iron
inside the swiftest hare
inside the flightiest duck
inside an egg.
It is inside that egg
you will find
the needle
and inside the needle
my very soul's gleam.

Can you trust me?
That I wish to be broken,
to be set upon by age?
You, who have always known
what it is to be known.

buried treasure
introductions
that take a lifetime

Largesse

Where does it begin, this imperative
to detect and meet the need in others?

The first time a baby places a hand
against their mother's salt-licked cheek
applying just enough pressure
to restart her world, to allay her fears
of a counter-clockwise life.

Those predestined teachers who tried
to channel our teenage angst
into concrete or abstract callings;
the tantalising possibility of both.
Who in deference to our half-hearted
death wishes   kept   on   teaching.

The girl least likely who allowed me
to tease her without reprisal until
I recognised myself in her most awkward
gestures of friendship.

Mistaking destitution for freedom
we hung out in the park after dark
where we were fed barbecued offcuts
and ghost stories by the truly homeless
until we remembered where we came from
        who we owed.

In his last will and testament, Shakespeare,
whoever he was when he was at home,
left his wife his second-best bed
and because history is always skewed
one way or another, we cannot know
if this was a snub or a final token of love.

This past year I've kept a chapbook of poems
on hand, in my bag, in my coat pocket –
thumbed and flipped and folded until
its cover image faded to apparition.
I want to impress upon the poet
I meant no disrespect.
That the relationship was as real as any.
That for a time what they gave utterly
confirmed me.

hand-me-downs
I hold them to me
invisible mends

Cause and effect

If at just that moment you
(daddy longlegs) had veered
some other way and not the way
of my keyboard where nothing
was happening
but where my fingers rested
anyway out of habit,
I might not have wondered …

All my life I have been naming you
wrongly: star of phobias,
Halloween decor, superhero.
You are more closely related
to the scorpion, the mite even.
No silk-glanded webspinner then.
Eight legs yes, but fragile as time.
And just the two eyes   like me.

At last count your kind was
four hundred million years old.
Give or take.

Oh ancient one! What do I know?

This –

You crawled the alphabet to disappear
inside a man's dressing gown.
The man rose slowly from the table
carefully undressing though it was
a cool enough autumn morning
and just yesterday there had been
a sprinkle of mountain snow.

And this –

When the man sat back down
in his singlet and shorts and waited
to see if you would reemerge,
whole, it was then, one thing leading
to another, that I was reminded
of his kindness –

vowed to love it more fiercely.

unconditional
the way she guards her sac
of spiderlings

A short history of the smile

'There are some people who raise their upper lip so high...that their teeth are almost entirely visible. This is entirely contradictory to decorum, which forbids you to allow your teeth to be uncovered, since nature gave us lips to conceal them.' – Jean-Baptiste De La Salle, http://www.scribd.com/doc/59273314/Christian-Decorum-Reprint-2007"\t"_blank The Rules of Christian Decorum and Civility, 1703

'French neurologist Guillaume-Benjamin-Amand Duchenne wanted to determine how the muscles in the human face produce facial expressions which he believed to be directly linked to the soul of man. He is known, in particular, for the way he triggered muscular contractions with electrical probes.' – Wikipedia

The first began
as a monkey fear grin
nonthreatening
(at the time).

Aeons later and
decorum be damned.

France 1835 shocked
the (almost) genuine
Duchenne one.

By the next century
the first laughter club
launched in India.

In preparation
for the Beijing Olympics
medal presenters
clenched chopsticks
cheek to cheek.

Under orders
Russian border guards
homour tourists
with the duty smile.

The laconic and the sardonic
each require a mirroring of sorts
if any ground is to be gained.

Embarrassed ones avert
their owner's eyes
angle the face
a self-deprecating
slope to the left.

Economies and excesses
take off our hats;
Ah the *Mona Lisa*…
The Cheshire Cat!

But pity the timorous
just shy of gigglehoood –
misjudged misunderstood

also the vacuous
those cut and paste deceptions
doomed as they are
to repeat without lesson.

family album
conflicting stories
behind smiles

The white tufted air

In a scene from a TV detective drama, one woman
plays the minor major part of petting a rabbit, as she
is routinely questioned about a murder we are led
to believe has almost nothing to do with her.

One hand restrains just as the other pacifies.

And if we were to pay as much attention to this
movement of metronomic fingers through fur
as trying to decipher whodunnit, we would perhaps
notice the way her hold loosens a little more with each
head-to-tail stroke, the vicarious comfort we find there.

We are struck instead by the policeman's involuntary
shudder as he turns to take his leave, as he/we witness
the final caress and snapping of the neck. For the pot
the woman reasonably explains, still, we swallow hard.

Later, discussing how best to hide our own creaturely scents,
to gain through cunning what we lack in speed and strength,
we try to map the chase, mark the safest point to circle back,
resume our colonised place.

But alone, how we spasm through sleep, now fearing above all
else the pacifier's gaze, her merciful hand unhurrying the pulse
we have come to trust, until all that's left separating
acquiescence from wildness is a single leap into the white
tufted air.

twilight
your face not so different
from mine

Meeting the man from the future

We meet by chance one autumn evening
the wind blowing intermittent gusts propelling
old gold leaves along the street outside a pub
named for whalers who drank there centuries
before and where now the man from the future
takes my hand, raises and kisses it lightly.
He is telling me the earth and the moon
are lovers, the whales too and the ghosts
of whales. His intelligence is at turns sharp
and tender, one minute a clear challenge
to preconception, the next shot through,
all reason escaping beneath a bifocal fog.
Homesick, he waxes lyrical about where
and when he's from, the ease of light rail
between the tenses. Though he admits
he's stuck at present – a small glitch –
and I find myself nodding a kind of collusion
because we can only imagine what we don't yet know:
the pub behind us serving good old days on tap,
the light ahead seeming to bend just so.

Bruny Island shack
the white wallaby shapes
our ghost stories

Surviving your imagined death

An unfamiliar presence lodges in your lower back,
digging in its teeth. It has teeth. For weeks you believe
you are dying and you keep this belief from me.

Concern skyrockets, plummets to dread, you bury it
beyond my reach, under layers of attentiveness
where you suggest longer country drives, dining out.

Every look you give me tinged with a sadness
I cannot understand because I do not yet know
the secret of your imagined death. How it informs

your every move: the way you reregister the car
for just six months, speak only in the present tense.
One day between gulps of winter air and Dutch ale,

you confess your fear. Name it. And in that moment
skin thins to intrusion. A glimpse of the abyss
of life without you; curls of hair falling and falling –

rhetorical question marks, unsolvable cryptograms.
In that moment a twisted wish for the simpler
explanation of   the other woman.

I give myself over to the eradication of ants.
Kneading bread dough. Suspending belief.
Anything for a rerun of normal. Of boring.

When the test results show the discs of your spine
nibbled by age but not cancer, we breathe out.
I resume knitting your birthday vest, a basket weave

in Oxblood Red. My Rumpelstiltskin hands working
each row like a mantra. All I yield. All I yield
               will sustain us.

first love letter
in perpetuity
the word hello

(I) Confirm humanity

(by not clicking the check box)

But by way of being this breath
    elemental   conceivable
           spore-like.

By way of rare and habitual song.

By way of moving my body
in tune seasonally in love.

By way of speaking by design
light-filled words without end.

By way of this hand in that.

By way of scars whose origins
I own and admonish and pardon.

By way of depth of sorrow breadth of joy.

By way of honoring rainmakers stargazers
keepers of story and promise and faith.

By way of the heart's defiant trajectory
looping back on itself across the fissures.

By way of my nature both real and imagined
both creaturely and eternally seraphic...

dear facebook friend
I could bump into you
without knowing

Simply 21

Wearing white is all it takes
for memory to snag me
like some dopey fish,
for the decades to slip and settle
into the low key center
of my twenty-first.

A sister just old enough
(with parental permission)
our friendship in the wings
biding time, gaining trust.
A brother who had yet to make
the worst kind of bad choice,
his vanity still a stranger
to mutant cells.

A baby (incredibly mine)
somewhere in the background,
perfect dreamless sleep
hers alone.
A husband I would take back
twice in five years then
never again.

Friends loyally fixed in time,
celebrating
in the flattering light.
Conflicting truths unimaginable.

It was 1985.
Someone gave me a bottle
of Kahlua.
Pop music was trying to feed
Ethiopia.

A hole in the ozone layer
had just been discovered.
Orwell's year of Big Brother
had come and gone
and stayed.

I could not know then
how much of life is spent
striving to bridge the gaps
between the tenses,
between the indefinite wait
to grow up
and the missed opportunity
of a blinked eye.

I was simply twenty-one,
between perms,
a coral pink smile rising
above the collar of my white
cheesecloth dress.

midwinter visit
the first of my childhood friends
to be orphaned

Diversional therapy

I scan the café's laminate tabletop, willing my predecessor
to gift me from the pages of an abandoned crossword
but I am the first absent-minded doodler of the day.
The newspaper before me mechanically folded,
woefully pristine. The Planes, Trains and Cars
colouring book merely a tease of motion.

Without the tool of my trade I am less myself;
a ballerina off point, a sniffer dog with anosmia.
What to do but beg?

Looking up from the salad bar as if it is a question
he has never been asked, ponytailed and tie-dyed
the waiter offers hope in the form of a barely concealed
caveat – this pen he undertones is my one and only.

And this serves to divert me further, duty bound now
to expedite whatever it is I simply must write,
the original seed of which is already dissipating,
shape-shifting into what else but a study of the implement
itself. The way the faded hotel name begins in a golden C
and ends in the breaking bite of someone else's eureka moment.
There is a disconcerting wobble and a vague stickiness
I cannot think on. Overall too thick for comfort but
an optimistic superhero-green (think Ninja Turtles).

Now and then its rightful owner looks over as if
to make sure I haven't left the country or found the secret
imbedded button which if pressed with just the right
lightness of touch could send me rocketing back or
forward to a time and place where everything revels
in its element: the sauerkraut, tabouli, writers and their pens –
the next great work just a few more short orders away.

table for one
what is my waiter
waiting for?

How it ends and begins

When he told her to go to hell
she said she would rather be
in hell than with him.
This is how she tells it sitting
smoking with a friend now,
relating the story of how it ended,
a nervous giggle between
nervous puffs. The friend looking
all the right ways: shocked, impressed,
just a little incredulous.
It could be she's heard it all before
this tug of warring words;
the last word followed by the wait to see
who will be the first to cave
under pressure of absence. And so it goes
the toing and froing, it's the way
of some unions, ill-equipped to settle
without threat of singledom ever testing
the gap between chasm and bond
between routine's delayed rewards
and the fraught spark of starting over.

gossiping
about herself
the chain smoker

Men I have worked for

(after Brendan Ryan's 'Men I have worked with')

The financier turned chook farmer I babysat for, who introduced me to divorce, stepchildren and the Moody Blues.

The supervisor who stood behind me at the assembly line offering to promote me to office girl after running his hand across the top of my Grace Jones haircut.

My father-in-law who demoted me from trade assistant to kitchen hand then closed his eyes against his son as I massaged his shoulders.

The dairy owner who gave me all the second chances he never had when I drove his tractor into the boundary fence and trapped the bull in the milking shed.

The frozen food man I worried would dock my pay for each icy fish I let slip through my fingers.

The mixed business man whose wife made prize-winning sponge cakes and looked at me sideways when her semi-precious went missing.

The caravan park manager who offered to pay me for a day's work as a domestic in cash or an evening of fine dining – my choice.

The café owners who reminded me to smile until my face was no longer my own.

The strawberry grower who allowed me to wheel myself between the rows with my toddler in my lap, grazing as we worked.

The ex-military officer I cooked for who wanted to know where my wild imagination and almond eyes came from.

The social worker who advised me to use my harrowed heart as a one-way ticket to anywhere else.

a book in my bag
answering the question
what do you do

Bringing the world home

Once I start it's impossible to stop
bringing the world home.

Beyond garish fridge magnets,
a falsehood of postcards,
logoed T-shirts from countries
      all made in China –

this more intimate memorabilia:

a pocket knife, silver coin taped
to its handle in a civil nod to superstition,

wooden love heart dotted with white
painted flowers because it was
my birthday in a language other than
and I reminded someone of his mother.

What the senses miss imagination allows for:

The neighbour's tiled roof glimpsed
through gauze curtains just as I'm waking,
not yet awake. One squint and I'm back
in Venice but where's the alley cat?

Graffiti on any underpass and a townhouse
next to a railway line revives something
of Chicago but alas no snow.

Mingling scents of tobacco and canine
transport me to a bar in Prague
and resistance to certain change.

Tracked across my dreamscape
these imprints of otherness, of usness.

Sleepwalking I follow each one
just a heartbeat from home.

eucalyptus oil
the airline pillow infused
with dreams of home

The naming

As the couple at the next table
rise to leave and he moves
to steady her walking frame
and she rebuffs him gently
with a coded tilt of her head
their baby names debate
culminates in a unified cry
of Leah! Princess Leah! Yeah!
It's a Star Wars reference
and I resist the temptation
to correct spelling, pronunciation
knowing my pedantry is small fry
alongside the inferred wish list
of attributes:
Their granddaughter-to-be
born leader
equal parts warrior and diplomat
striding forth
liberated from her metal bikini,
the nickname Your Worshipfulness
a tender tease barely touching
the magnitude of their galactic love.
Such is the power –
they allow themselves to believe –
of naming.

baby name book
crossing off
the worst rhymes

The facts of our lives

Once he had sold one too many suburban life sentences
my father moved us to the country to raise chickens
which didn't seem to make him any happier but at least
he was his own man and no rooster to speak of...

Grandma Moses was seventy-eight when she launched
a career in folk art immortalising apple butter and
the quilting bee.

The husband of my childhood friend approaching sixty
tells me he has been daydreaming of walking away
from his university position to become a tram driver
to track the streets of his city day in day out knowing
and not knowing what lies just around the next bend.

The father of a boy I once cared for left the public service
midlife to apprentice himself to his wife the furniture maker;
to speak the same language differently, more tenderly alert
perhaps to the best and worst of it – the warp and weathering
mindful measuring of the boxed heart.

One day you are shucking oysters for a living, the next
auditioning as a stand-up comedian because oyster shucking
has given you so much fine material to work with.

But wait there's more!

Defence lawyers who moonlight as method actors.

Infamous spies turned world-class pastry chefs.

Accountants delivering pitch-perfect sing-o-grams.

A pop star with a PhD in gerontology.

And on his days off from the live bait and tackle shop
the boy who never caught a fish he didn't return is finally learning
how to swim – backward forward – first the dead man's float then
rhythmic   breathing   between   the   strokes.

Each day we get on with proving them, the facts of our lives.
Each night teased by growing pains, we strain our seams,
mutable beings
all.

his ninetieth year
my father buys
my mother a house

Letting in the neighbour

Insect heat drives us to leave
the bedroom window open
despite the all-night party
a few houses down.

The night is abuzz with stridulation,
jazzy piano, deeply sourced bass…

Near the witching hour we discover
the occasion is Sarah. We know this
because of the birthday song
followed by a silence
peppered with audience laughter
during the thank you speech.

So. We know her first name but not her last,
her birthdate but not her age,
that she can be funny, is popular, that her taste
in music runs to improvisation, syncopation –
cool earthy grooves.

Early next morning we walk the streets
trying to guess but the houses
are conspiratorially staid, each one
in silent cahoots with its neighbour,
the mouths of letter boxes firmly closed.

Not even a surreptitious glimpse in the recycled
gives it up – the door behind which a gentle force
field holds her   Sarah   whoever she is
sleeping off another stellar act between the ages.

suburban fog
a pumpkin flowers through
my neighbour's fence

Present tense

A man walks into a bar looking for an audience.
The beginning of anything is always part re-
enactment part projection. This is merely my
version of events.

A man walks into a charity shop looking like
he's looking for a close encounter of the fifth kind.
He dances barefoot at the mercy of Vincent
de Paul whose father traded the family oxen
for a spirit guide for his teenage son
which could be seen as a good or bad omen
depending on your type and level of hunger.

Winter-damp tracksuit pants hemmed in mud he
whirligigs among us as we stalk the pleats
and plaids of our retrofitted bygone days.

When he speaks he claims in one breath:
interminable weather, a recent mugging and
a not so distant relation to Fred Astaire.

We are trading there but for the grace smiles
when the heavily inked sales girl approaches
asking if Sir would be after some trousers today?
A jacket perhaps? Some shoes? As if this were
a high-end fashion store that doesn't do irony.

When he exits stage left, classically dressed,
the small bow he leaves us with somehow
makes it easier to believe the gods
were once in love with the idea of us.
That in our beginning we were each
singular and transparent as the first teardrop
travelling along the first tear duct.

That we have more to offer than this collage
of snakeskin snapshot through an eyeful
of palm tree between venetian blinds, sitting
on some holiday balcony casually crossing
one leg over the other as if we have all the time
in the world to wait for the ticker-tape parade,
the transmigration of wind through our wishbones,
perfect strangers lifting the veil on our lives
nodding their not quite but almost familial assent
saying go on then love give us a twirl…

window-shopping
one by one the charities
go retro

I try to not write a pandemic poem and fail

Because without context I fear we will remain strangers miserly growing our personal space.

Because children colouring in the bricks of their suburban home until it looks like a rainbow Rubik's cube is suddenly newsworthy.

Because I stopped for a while and now I have started again.

Because the supermarket checkout operator behind the Perspex shield insists more than ever that I have a good day.

Because my sister tells me she found God in anger management class and there is no punchline, only the knot of a smile unravelling.

Because as the tiny purple grapes from a neighbour's vine burst on my tongue I feel our kinship deepen.

Because any day now bread and poetry could become legal tender.

Because if looking is the new way of touching I want you to know I see you. I do.

Because when people who are not musicians need to make music they remember the wooden spoons and saucepan lids of childhood and have at it.

Because I am silenced by the sign language of everything.

Because the sun will not stop or the moon or the birds.

Because I am hardwired to respond.

hopeful
my neighbour sanitises
her letter box

Like Alice letting go

My hair once golden
sheaves of wheat danced
in the rabbitty air as I fell.
Much later in the right hands
it could be stroked alight.
As my sight begins streaming
inward I listen more closely
for the music of flowers,
the pulse of sun and moon
at my throat.
These are things
only the imagination
can fathom. Also
a candle flame
after the flame is blown out
and the weight of the earth's
metallic heart.
The world is full of curios
at every turn.
Let it be said I never stopped
wondering…

on a good day
the bucket list
empty

www.ingramcontent.com/pod-product-compliance
Lightning Source LLC
Chambersburg PA
CBHW070924080526
44589CB00013B/1416